The Fables of

AESOP

THE FABLES OF

AESOP

Selected and Illustrated by

DAVID LEVINE

Translated by

Patrick and Justina Gregory

Dorset Press
New York

FOR MILDRED

This edition published by Dorset Press
a division of Marboro Books Corporation,
by arrangement with Harvard Common Press
1989 Dorset Press

ISBN 0-88029-434-5

Printed in the United States of America
M 9 8 7 6 5 4 3 2 1

Contents

The first fable in each of the following pairs corresponds to the illustration on the opposite page.

Fables   Illustrations

About Aesop
and This Translation

The best, because most nearly contemporary, information on the life of Aesop comes from Herodotus. From him we learn that Aesop the fabulist lived in the first half of the sixth century B.C., was the slave of a wealthy Samian, and was murdered by the citizens of Delphi. Later writers have filled in this outline and elaborated a legend. Aristotle reports that Aesop instructed the people of Samos in the art of politics by reciting his fables; Plutarch turns Aesop into a traveling ambassador for King Croesus of Lydia; and a late *Life of Aesop* describes him as the ugliest of men, with a snub nose, thick lips, pot belly, knock knees, and a pronounced stoop. The accounts of his death vary in detail, but they generally agree that while visiting the Oracle at Delphi he fell afoul of the local inhabitants and was put to death on a trumped-up charge of impiety. At least one author attributes this murder to Aesop's satirical talent, which was not appreciated by the Delphians when exercised at their expense.

Ancient biography does not generally attempt, or even desire, accuracy, and much of this information is undoubtedly every bit as fanciful as it sounds. But it seems likely that Aesop did indeed exist, and that his name is not just a label attached to a collection of fables. Of Aesop's influence in antiquity there can be no doubt. The Athenians erected a statue to him; Aristophanes cites him repeatedly, and Socrates spent his final days in prison turning Aesop's fables into verse. In the fourth century B.C., Demetrius of Phalerum put together a prose collection of the fables of Aesop, and it is from this collection that all later versions seem ultimately to derive.

We have based our English versions on the Greek text published in the Société des Belles Lettres edition of Emile Chambry. We have done our best to reproduce in English the precision and spareness that characterize these prose fables and make them somewhat different in tone from later, more elaborate retellings. On the whole, we have found that the fewer words we could get away with, the truer to the original our versions seemed.

We have deliberately departed from the Greek text in one respect: by deleting the summarizing morals that appear at the end of most of the fables. Although this omission was wholly arbitrary on our part, it is not without precedent. The morals are in some cases later additions to the fables; and even Chambry admits that they "often have only a vague connection with the fable, and on occasion none at all." It seems to us that these moral tags not only jar with the fables' sophistication of form, but also deprive them of one of their prime functions: to make the reader think. The world of the fables is not a judicial system of mistakes made and lessons learned; it is a place permeated with a spirit of ambiguity and presided over by the Socratic maxim, "Know thyself!" It seemed best, therefore, to omit the morals and leave the fables to speak for themselves.

PATRICK AND JUSTINA GREGORY

The Fables

The Lion, the Ass, and the Fox

The Lion, the Ass, and the Fox went hunting together. Their luck was good, and at the end of the day the Lion asked the Ass to divide up the spoils. The Ass divided everything into three equal portions and invited the Lion to take his pick, whereupon the indignant Lion leaped upon the Ass and devoured him on the spot. He then turned to the Fox and invited him to make a new division. The Fox hastily piled everything into one great heap, save for a few odd scraps, and asked the Lion to choose. The Lion asked the Fox who had taught him to divide so well.

"The Ass," replied the Fox.

The Ass and the Lapdog

The owner of an Ass also had a little Lapdog. The Dog was a firm favorite, and whenever the man returned from dining out, he would never forget to bring back some tidbit, which he tossed to the Dog, who leapt about him gaily, wagging his tail. The Ass looked upon these performances with eager eyes, and one day, on his master's return, he began to gambol about him and accidently kicked the man. Furious, the master beat the Ass soundly and locked him in the stable.

The Cat and the Birds

A Cat, hearing that there were some sick Birds in the neighborhood, got himself up as a doctor and set off to pay a house call. When he arrived at their home he called out to ask how the occupants were getting on.

"Very well, thank you," came the reply, "if only you would go away."

The Woman Married to a Drunkard

A Woman had a Drunkard for a husband. To cure him of his habit she devised the following scheme. One day when he was dead drunk she hoisted him upon her shoulders, carried him to the cemetery, and deposited him within the walls. When she judged that the effects of the drink had begun to wear off, she returned to the cemetery and knocked at the gate. "Who's there?" called the Drunkard. "It's the man who brings food for the dead," his wife replied. "It's not food we need," cried her husband, "but drink. Here I am, dead of thirst, and you talk of food!" The Woman beat her breast and exclaimed: "Alas, my attempt at a cure has only made you worse, for what was once a vice now seems to have become part of your nature."

The Fox and the Goat

A Fox fell into a well and could not get out. A thirsty Goat peered over the edge, and on seeing the Fox down there asked whether the water was good to drink. The Fox, hiding his distress, eloquently extolled the quality of the water and invited the Goat to join him. The Goat, at the risk of his neck, managed to clamber down, and, after drinking his fill, consulted with the Fox as to the best way of getting out again. "It is easy if we help each other," said the Fox. "Just brace your forelegs against the side and raise your head up high. I will climb over you, and when I have gotten out I will pull you up." The Goat willingly agreed to the plan and the Fox, having used the Goat's shoulder, head, and horns as a ladder, scrambled over the side of the well and promptly disappeared from sight. When the Goat berated him for not keeping his side of the agreement, the departing Fox called back: "Look here, Friend, if your head was good for anything besides sprouting horns, you would have known better than to get into a well without having a way to get out."

The Cowardly Hunter and the Woodcutter

A Hunter asked a Woodcutter whether he had seen any lion tracks in the area. "Matter of fact," replied the Woodcutter, "I can lead you right to the lion himself." At this the Hunter turned pale and stammered: "It's . . . it's the tracks I'm looking for, not . . . not the lion."

The Fox and the Leopard

The Fox and the Leopard were each boasting of his beauty. The Leopard kept coming back to the intricate design of his coat, until the Fox finally declared: "But I am surely more beautiful than you — for it is my mind that is intricate, not merely my pelt."

The Bat, the Bramblebush, and the Gull

A Bat, a Bramblebush, and a Gull decided to form a business partnership. The Bat borrowed money to finance the enterprise, the Bramblebush invested in cloth, and the Gull contributed a quantity of copper ingots. They then set out by ship to sell their wares abroad. On route, their ship ran into a violent storm and capsized; and though the three partners managed to escape with their lives, all their goods were lost. Ever since, the Gull has hovered around the seacoast, hoping that some of his copper will be washed ashore by the waves; the Bat, fearful of his creditors, has kept well hidden during the day, venturing out only at dusk; and the Bramblebush plucks at the garments of passers-by, to see if any of the cloth really is his.

The Fox and the Grapes

A hungry Fox spotted some Grapes dangling plump and ripe from a vine overhead. Though he stood on his hind legs and stretched forth his long muzzle, he still could not reach them. As he slunk away he was heard to remark: "Those Grapes are probably sour anyway."

The Eagle, the Jackdaw, and the Shepherd

An Eagle swooped down from his mountain perch and carried off a young lamb A Jackdaw, who had witnessed the scene, was dazzled by the Eagle's performance and determined to emulate it. With a loud croak he landed on the back of a ram, but his claws got tangled in the thick wool and he beat his wings in vain. The Shepherd came running, grabbed hold of the bird, and clipped his wings. That evening he took him home to his children as a pet. When his children asked him what kind of a bird he had brought them, the Shepherd replied: "Well, as far as I can tell it's a simple Jackdaw, but he seems to think that he's an Eagle."

The Fox Who Had Lost His Tail

A Fox who had lost his Tail in a trap was so ashamed of his appearance that he found life unbearable. He determined to persuade the other foxes to cut off their tails so as to transform his personal infirmity into a social convention. With this in mind he called a meeting of all the foxes and urged them to rid themselves of their tails which — he declared — were ugly appendages and a burden to carry about. But one of the foxes interrupted him, saying: "Look brother, you wouldn't be giving us this advice if there weren't something in it for you."

The Lion and the Wild Ass

A Lion and a Wild Ass went hunting together, the Lion contributing his strength, the Wild Ass his speed. At the end of the day the Lion divided the spoils into three parts. "The first part," he explained, "belongs to me, as King of the Beasts, and the second part is my due as a partner in this enterprise. As for the third part, it is sure to bring you bad luck if you so much as touch it, so I advise you to get out of here this minute!"

The Eagle and the Dung Beetle

An Eagle was after a hare. The desperate hare ran up to the only creature in sight, a little Dung Beetle, and implored his help. The Dung Beetle promised his support, and when the Eagle swooped down he informed the great bird that the hare was under his protection and was not to be molested. The Eagle, however, could not be bothered with such a lowly creature and devoured the hare before the Dung Beetle's very eyes. From that time on the Dung Beetle bore no love for the Eagle. He kept a close watch on the great bird's nest, and whenever the Eagle laid any eggs, the Dung Beetle would manage to roll them out of the nest so they broke on the rocks below. The Eagle, unable to cope with these tactics, finally appealed to Zeus (for the Eagle is sacred to Zeus) and begged him to provide a safe refuge for her brood. The god graciously allowed the Eagle to lay her eggs in his lap. When the Dung Beetle saw what was going on, he formed a plan. Making a little ball of dung, he took flight and dropped it into Zeus's lap. The god jumped up to shake off the dung, and in so doing inadvertently flung away the Eagle's eggs. Ever since then, they say, the Eagle never lays eggs during Dung Beetle season.

The Jackdaw and the Fox

A hungry Jackdaw alighted on the branch of a fig tree, and seeing that the figs were still green, he decided to wait there until they ripened. A Fox, fascinated by the Jackdaw's long vigil, asked what he was doing, and then said: "Don't fool yourself, my friend. You can feed on hopes, but they won't make you fat!"

The Fisherman and the Minnow

A Fisherman hauled in his net to find nothing but a Minnow. The Minnow begged him, out of consideration for his small size, to throw him back into the water.

"Just think!" said the Minnow, "one day I will have grown into a great big fish, and then when you haul me in, you'll really have got something!"

"Seems to me," replied the Fisherman, "that I'd be a damn fool to give up what I've got *now*, for something I haven't got *yet*, no matter how big."

The Old Lion and the Fox

An Old Lion found that he could no longer support himself by hunting and decided to get his food by trickery. He retired to a cave and sent out word that he was near death. When the animals came to pay their last respects, he seized them and ate them up. Many had perished in this way when the Fox came by. He stopped some distance from the cave and called out to ask how the Lion was feeling. "Poorly, very poorly," replied the Lion, who then invited the Fox to pay him a visit inside his cave. "I'd be glad to," said the Fox, "except for one thing: I can see signs that many animals have entered your cave, but none that any of them have ever come out!"

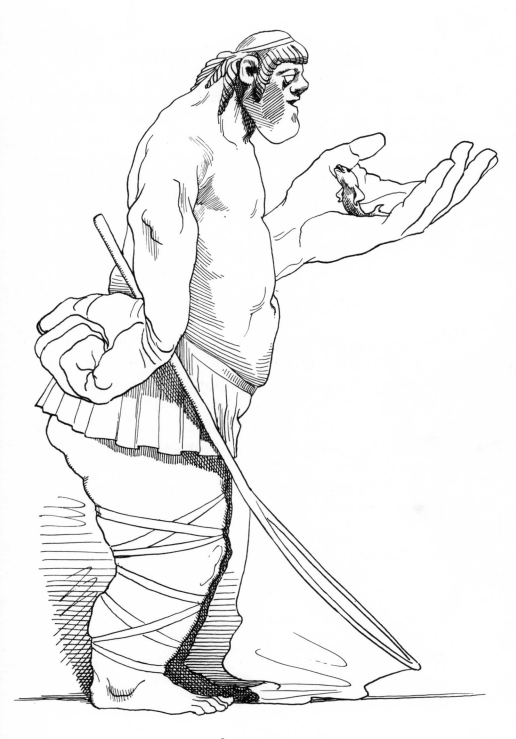

The Rich Athenian in Distress

A Rich Athenian was on a sea voyage when the boat ran into a violent storm and capsized. While the other passengers set out to swim to shore, the Rich Athenian paddled about in the water, imploring Athena's aid and promising her all sorts of fine offerings if only she would save him. A fellow passenger who was swimming alongside managed to call out: "Look to Athena if you like, but look to your arms as well!"

Heracles and Ploutos

When Heracles was first raised to Mount Olympus and given the privilege of eating with the gods, he made sure to greet each of his dinner companions as they came in with courtesy and warmth. Last of all Ploutos, the god of wealth, came in to the dining hall — and Heracles turned his back and pretended not to notice him. Zeus, surprised at this rudeness, took Heracles aside to ask why he had singled Ploutos out for such ill treatment.

"When I was living among men," said Heracles, "I noticed that Ploutos kept company with the worst sort of people."

The Man Who Promised the Impossible

A poor Man lay very ill. The doctors despaired of saving him, so he addressed himself to the gods, and vowed to give them a hundred head of oxen as well as endless golden offerings if only they would restore him to health. His wife, who was at his bedside, was bewildered by these vows and asked him, "How do you ever expect to pay for all that?" He replied: "Do you really think that I would be so foolish as to make such promises if there were any chance that I might have to fulfill them?"

The Ugly Slave Girl and Aphrodite

An ugly, unscrupulous Slave Girl captured the affections of her master. With the money he gave her she decked herself out so as to rival her own mistress in splendor. She never forgot to make offerings to Aphrodite and to pray the goddess to make her beautiful. Finally, however, Aphrodite appeared to her one night in a dream and declared: "I have no intention of making you beautiful, for I am angry at that man who insists on seeing beauty in such as you."

The Astronomer

An Astronomer was in the habit of wandering out at night to examine the stars. One evening, on the outskirts of town, he fell into a well. A passerby heard his cries for help and upon learning what had happened remarked: "Well, friend, it seems you can see the heavens clear enough, but can't see what's right at your feet."

The Lion and the Bull

A Lion had long feasted his eyes on a very large Bull but could think of no way of overpowering him except by trickery. He sent word to the Bull that he had recently slaughtered a fine plump lamb and would like his friend to share in the feast. (The Lion's intention was to leap on the Bull while his guest was reclining at table.)

The Bull arrived at the Lion's lair and saw before him a grand array of enormous cooking pots and a long spit extended over a great open fire. Having taken in the scene, he turned on his hoofs and started off home. The Lion called after him, protesting that he had suffered no harm and had no cause to leave such a delectable dinner untasted.

"I have cause enough," was the reply. "These cooking preparations are far more appropriate for a very large Bull than for a fine plump lamb."

The Herdsman and the Lion

A Herdsman was driving his cattle to pasture when he noticed that one of his calves was missing. After searching everywhere and in vain, he turned to Zeus and vowed to sacrifice a kid if only the god would lead him to the creature who stole his calf. A short time later he entered a dense forest and suddenly found himself face to face with a huge Lion who was busy devouring a calf. The terrified Herdsman raised his arms to the heavens and pleaded: "Oh great Zeus, I promised you a kid in return for leading me to whoever was robbing my herd; now I am offering you a bull if you will save me from the robber!"

Heracles and Athena

Heracles was making his way along a narrow road when he saw on the ground an object that looked like an apple. He stepped on it and the object doubled in size. Seeing this, Heracles stamped on it with both feet and hit it with his club. The object then swelled in size until it blocked the road. Heracles threw down his club and gaped in amazement. Athena now appeared and said to him: "Leave that thing alone, dear brother! It is the spirit of argument and discord; if you don't touch it, it does no harm, but if you try to fight with it, it grows as you have seen."

The Cat and Aphrodite

A Cat fell in love with a handsome young man and petitioned Aphrodite to change her into a woman. The goddess sympathized with her plight and transformed her into a beautiful young girl who won the young man's heart at first sight. On their wedding night Aphrodite, curious to see whether the transformation was more than skin deep, let loose a mouse in the nuptial chamber. The Cat, wholly forgetting who and where she was, leaped out of bed and set out after the mouse. The indignant goddess thereupon changed her back to her original form.

The Doe and the Vine

A Doe, pursued by hunters, hid herself behind a Grapevine. When the hunters had passed, she tranquilly began to nibble the leaves, thinking herself safe; but the hunters, who happened to look back, saw the leaves trembling and guessed that an animal was lurking there. As the Doe felt death upon her she exclaimed: "I only got what I deserved, for I should not have harmed the Vine that served me so well."

The Middle-aged Man
and His Two Mistresses

A Middle-aged Man had Two Mistresses, one young and lovely, the other well past her prime. The older woman, embarrassed by having a lover younger than herself, would pluck out the black hairs from his head whenever she was with him. The younger woman, ashamed at being seen with an aging lover, would pluck out the gray hairs. And so it was that between the two of them, the Middle-aged Man soon became bald.

Man's First Sight of the Camel

The first Men to see a Camel were terrified by its great size and took to their heels. In time, however, they came to realize that the Camel is by nature a gentle creature and they no longer feared to approach him. Finally, when they noticed that nothing could make him lose his temper, Men held the Camel in such scorn that they put a bridle on him and allowed their children to lead him about.

The Farmer and the Poisonous Snake

A Poisonous Snake bit a Farmer's child and the child died. The Farmer, overcome by grief and rage, took his axe and set up a vigil outside the Snake's hole, ready to strike the creature down as soon as it emerged. Eventually the Snake put his head out of the hole and the Farmer struck; but the blow missed its mark, splitting in two the rock that stood at the entrance to the Snake's home. The Farmer now thought it prudent to revise his plan and sought to make peace with the Snake. But the Snake said: "We can never be friends with such reminders of our enmity always before our eyes — for me, the split rock; for you, your child's tombstone."

The Shepherd and the Sea

A Shepherd who was pasturing his sheep along the seacoast looked out over the calm waters and decided to try his hand at commerce. He sold his sheep, bought a shipload of dates, and set sail to sell them abroad. A violent storm arose, and it was only by jettisoning his entire cargo that he managed to keep the ship from capsizing and to return to port. Some time later a man happened to admire the tranquil grandeur of the Sea, which at that moment was indeed wondrously calm, when the Shepherd interjected: "That's only because it wants more dates."

The Old Woman and the Doctor

An Old Woman was having trouble with her eyes and called in a Doctor, who prescribed a course of treatment. On every visit he would apply an ointment, and while her eyes were closed he would carry off some item of household furniture. When the house was completely stripped he declared her cured and presented his bill. The Old Woman refused to pay it, and the Doctor brought her into court. She admitted to the judge that she had agreed beforehand to pay the Doctor a certain sum if he succeeded in curing her; but since his visits, she complained, her sight had grown much worse. "Before," she said, "I could at least make out the furniture in my house; now I can't see a thing."

The Old Man and Death

An Old Man with a bundle of firewood on his back trudged along the road. He had come far and had a long way to go. Suddenly overcome by tiredness, he put down his load and sighed aloud for death. Suddenly, Death was there before him, asking why he had been called.

"Would you be so kind," said the Old Man, "to carry this bundle for me?"

Demedes the Politician

Demedes the Politician was haranguing the citizens of Athens. He noticed that their attention was wandering, so he asked permission to recount one of Aesop's fables, and began:

"Demeter, a Swallow and an Eel were traveling together. When they came to a river, the Swallow took flight, the Eel plunged into the water . . ." At this point he stopped.

"And what about Demeter?" came the cry from the crowd. "What did *she* do?

"She flew into a rage," replied Demedes, "because you neglect the affairs of State to listen to some silly fable!"

Zeus and Modesty

When Zeus had fashioned man and enclosed all his attributes within the mortal frame, he discovered that Modesty had been omitted. Distressed at his oversight, Zeus ordered Modesty to enter through the back door. After much protest, she agreed, but declared categorically that if anyone else used this entrance she would quit the residence for good. Which is why all buggers lack Modesty.

The Travelers and the Bear

Two friends were traveling together. As they went down a country road, they met a large Bear. One of the friends quickly climbed a tree and hid himself in the branches; the other man, who was slower afoot, lay down and pretended to be dead — for bears, it is said, will not touch a dead creature. The Bear ambled up and sniffed around the man's head, but the man held his breath and after a while the Bear took himself off. His friend, who had been watching from the tree, called out to ask whether the Bear had harmed him.

"Not at all," answered the man, "he just whispered something in my ear."

"And what was that?" asked his startled companion.

"Never travel with a friend who won't stand by you in danger," answered the other.

The Oxen and the Axle

Two Oxen were pulling a cart when the Axle began to creak. Turning their heads they exclaimed: *"We're* doing the work, and *you're* complaining!"

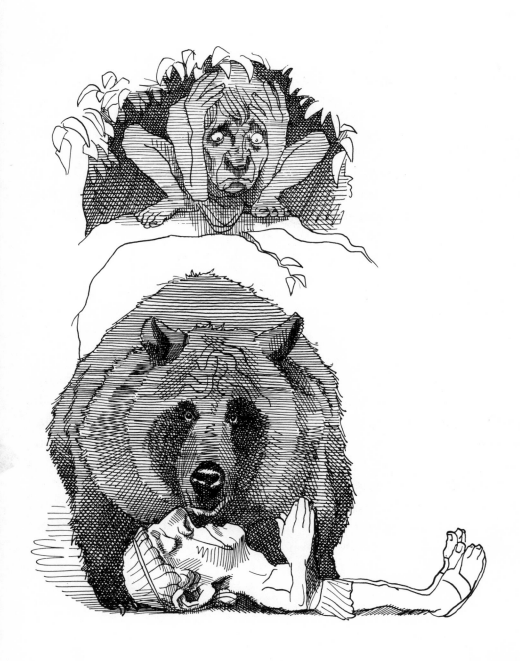

The Two Enemies

Two Enemies happened to be passengers on the same ship, and having recognized each other, withdrew to opposite ends of the vessel. In the middle of the voyage a terrible storm broke and the ship began to sink. When it became clear that everyone on board was doomed, the man in the stern asked the captain which end of the ship was likely to plunge into the waves first.

"The bow," answered the captain.

"Well then," said the man, "it will be worth it to see my Enemy die before I do."

The Ass and the Load of Salt

An Ass carrying a Load of Salt was fording a river when he slipped and fell into the water. The Salt on his back instantly dissolved, and the Ass, feeling his load lightened, emerged from the water delighted with his little accident. Some days later he arrived at the riverside laden with sponges, and thinking that he could rid himself of this load in the same way, he deliberately tumbled into the stream. But the sponges filled with water so that the Ass could not regain his footing and he drowned.

The Stag and the Lion

A Stag came to a pool and, after drinking his fill, paused to contemplate his image in the still water. The sight of his antlers in all their sturdy splendor filled him with pride, but his legs struck him as a sorry sight, frail and scrawny. While he was thus absorbed in his thoughts a Lion suddenly burst upon him. The Stag took flight, and quickly outdistanced the Lion — for a Stag's strength is in his legs, whereas a Lion's is in his heart. As long as he kept to the open ground he continued to outrun his pursuer, but when he entered a thick forest his antlers caught in the branches and the Lion gradually overtook him. As he was about to be killed, the Stag lamented to himself: "How strange is fate! Those pitiable legs of mine almost saved me, and my noble antlers have proved my undoing!"

The Fly

A Fly fell into the cookpot. As he was about to drown in the stew, he said to himself: "Well, I've eaten, I've drunk, and I've had my bath. Let death come, I'm ready for him."

The Hen That Laid Golden Eggs

A man had a Hen that laid Golden Eggs. Thinking that she must have a great nugget of solid gold inside her, he killed her and cut her open — only to find that she was no different within from other hens. And so it was that in hoping to gain a great fortune he lost a fine income.

The North Wind and the Sun

The North Wind and the Sun were arguing about which of them was the stronger. Finally they decided on a contest of strength, the winner being the one who could strip the clothes from the back of a passing wayfarer. The North Wind began; but the more fiercely he blew, the closer the traveler drew his clothes about him. And when the man began putting on additional garments against the cold, the North Wind gave up the struggle. The Sun then took over. He glowed gently, just above the horizon, until the man had shed the additional clothes; then he climbed higher and shone more brightly until the wayfarer, unable to bear the heat, stripped naked and plunged into a nearby river to bathe.

The Statue Vendor

A man carved a statue of Hermes out of wood and took it to market. The day wore on and no buyer appeared, so the man began to cry his wares, reminding everyone that Hermes was a god guaranteed to bring in both money and good luck. A passerby asked him: "Look here, if he's such a moneymaker, why do you want to get rid of him?" The Vendor replied: "The gods always take their time, and it so happens that I need cash right now."

The Man and the Lion

A Man and a Lion were traveling along the road together and each was boasting to the other of his great strength. At a turn in the road they came upon a statue of a man wrestling with a lion. The man was clearly getting the better of the struggle.

"You can see," said the Man, "that men are indeed stronger than lions."

"I can see," replied his companion, "that this statue was not carved by a lion."

The Ages of Man

When Zeus created Man, he made him short-lived. When winter came Man, making use of his intelligence, built himself a house; and one day a horse, who could no longer stand the freezing rain and cutting wind, came to the house and begged for shelter. The Man said that he would admit the horse on one condition: that he give him a portion of the years allotted to him by Zeus. The horse willingly agreed. A little later an ox appeared, driven to the house by the cruel weather. The Man demanded the same entrance fee from the ox, who paid without protest. Finally a dog, half-dead with cold, came by and yielded a number of his years in order to gain admittance. The result of these transactions was this: during the time allotted them by Zeus, Men are unspoiled and good; when they are using the years given by the horse they are proud and hard to manage; when they reach the years of the ox they are able leaders; and, at the end of their lives, having fallen back upon the dog years, they become ill-tempered scolds.

The Hares and the Foxes

Once upon a time the Hares, who were at war with the eagles, asked the Foxes to be their allies. The Foxes replied: "If only we did not know what you are, and what your enemies are, we would have been glad to help you."

Zeus and Men

Zeus shaped the bodies of Men and then instructed Hermes to infuse his creations with intelligence. Hermes divided the supply into equal portions and gave one portion to each man, regardless of his size. Thus it is that short, slight men are amply endowed with intelligence, whereas great, strapping fellows are understocked and generally stupid.

The Eagle with Clipped Wings and the Fox

One day an Eagle was caught by a man, who clipped his wings and tossed him in among the barnyard fowl. The Eagle was so stricken with grief and humiliation that he could not eat; he was like a king in chains. But he was sold to another man who plucked out the old feathers and rubbed the wings with myrrh, so the feathers grew back with renewed strength. As soon as the Eagle could fly again he chased down a hare and presented it to his new owner as a sign of his gratitude. A Fox who had watched the proceedings said to him: "You should have offered the gift to the first man, not the second. The second man is good-natured and will never do you harm, but the other is dangerous and you would do well to court him."

The Crow and the Fox

A Crow, having stolen a piece of meat, settled down with it on the branch of a tree. A passing Fox caught sight of him and made up his mind then and there to get the meat for himself. Gazing up into the branches, he exclaimed over the Crow — what a fine figure he was, how neat and elegant! "Surely," the Fox thought out loud, "this Crow deserves to be king of the birds — and he would be, if only he could sing." The Crow, anxious to show the Fox that he did indeed possess a voice, let out a loud croak — and the meat dropped to the ground.

"Ah Crow!" said the Fox as he rushed forward to claim the meat, "I see now that what you were lacking was not a voice, but good sense."

The Pig and the Sheep

A Pig happened to fall in among a herd of Sheep and decided to share their pasture with them. A few days later the shepherd seized hold of him, whereupon the Pig gave out such blood-curdling squeals that the Sheep were astonished and shocked. "He often takes hold of us," they said, "but we never carry on like that!" "It's all very well to say," replied the Pig, "but our cases are different: he grabs you for your wool, but with me it's my flesh he is after!"

The Dog and the Piece of Meat

A Dog with a Piece of Meat in his jaws was fording a river when he caught sight of his reflection in the water and mistook it for another dog with an even bigger piece of meat in his jaws. Instantly he dropped his own meat and sprang to the attack, and so he lost both what he had, and what he had not: for there was no other dog, and his meat was swept away by the strong current.

The Cat and the Mice

A house was infested with Mice. A Cat moved in and proceeded to catch the Mice one by one. The survivors finally took to their holes and refused to come out. The Cat's patience was severely tried, and he realized that he would have to think of some ruse to lure the Mice out of their shelters. And that is how he came to hang himself from a wooden beam, pretending to be dead. Finally one of the Mice peered out of his hole and exclaimed: "Look here, my friend, even if you were dead and buried I wouldn't come near your grave!"

The Gnat and the Bull

A Gnat settled on the horn of a Bull, and after resting there a good long time finally asked if the Bull would prefer him to depart. The Bull replied: "I didn't notice when you came; why should I notice when you go?"

The Lion, the Wolf, and the Fox

The Lion, old and ailing, was confined to his lair, and all the animals came to pay their respects — all, that is, except the Fox. The Wolf, seizing the opportunity, loudly denounced the Fox to the Lion. He asserted that the Fox had so little esteem for their common lord and master that he did not even deign to pay him a visit. The Fox entered on these final words and was greeted by an angry roar from the Lion. Having requested a moment to defend himself, the Fox said: "And who among all those assembled here can claim to be such a loyal servant to Your Majesty as I, who have traveled to all the doctors in the realm in search of a remedy for your illness — and found it!" The Lion commanded him to transmit the remedy immediately. The Fox replied: "You must wrap yourself in the still warm pelt of a freshly slaughtered Wolf." The Wolf was slaughtered on the spot, and the Fox was heard to cheerfully remark: "A master should always be encouraged to do deeds of mercy, not of spite."

The Lion and the Farmer's Daughter

The Lion fell in love with the Farmer's Daughter and asked for her hand in marriage. The Farmer did not like the idea of marrying his Daughter to a ferocious beast; nor, for that matter, did he like the idea of refusing him. He told the Lion that, though he considered him a son-in-law after his own heart, his Daughter was naturally alarmed by his long teeth and claws, and that he could not grant his consent to the marriage until the Lion had had both teeth and claws removed. Because the Lion was in love, he agreed to the double sacrifice. But when he appeared at the Farmer's cottage to claim his bride, he was greeted with scorn and driven away with a stout stick.

Zeus and the Tortoise

Zeus, who had just married, invited all the animals to his wedding party. Only the Tortoise failed to come. The next day Zeus sought him out and asked: "Why did you not attend my little celebration last night?" "Oh, you know," answered the Tortoise. "There's no place like home!" This reply so angered Zeus that he condemned the Tortoise to carry his home on his back ever after.

The Lion, the Bear, and the Fox

The Lion and the Bear came across a fawn in the forest and fell to fighting over who would have it. They fought hard and long until, overcome by wounds and exhaustion, they sank down on the ground. The Fox happened to be passing by, and seeing the two adversaries stretched out half-dead with the prize lying between them, he carried off the fawn before their very eyes. The two great beasts said to each other: "Was it for the sake of the Fox that we put ourselves to such pain and trouble?"

The Peacock and the Jackdaw

The birds were avidly discussing who should be their king. Into the center of the assembly strutted the Peacock, who spread wide his glorious tail and cried out that the honor was surely due to him because of his beauty. The birds were on the point of declaring him king when the Jackdaw spoke: "O Peacock, what use will your beauty be when the Eagle attacks us, and you are called upon to defend your subjects?"

The Lion and the Grateful Mouse

A Lion lay dozing when a Mouse scampered over his back. The Lion awoke with a start and seized the Mouse in his huge paw. The Mouse begged the Lion to save his life and promised, if released, to do as much for him someday. The Lion burst out laughing at the Mouse's ridiculous promise, but let him go. A little later it happened that the Lion was captured by some hunters and tied to a tree with a stout rope. The Mouse heard his roars, hurried to his side, and in a short time had gnawed through the rope and set the Lion free. "Not long ago," said the Mouse, "you laughed at the thought of my returning your favor. Now you know that mice can show gratitude."

The Wild Boar and the Fox

A Wild Boar was busily sharpening his tusks on the trunk of a tree. The Fox asked why he was putting himself to such trouble when there were no hunters in the vicinity and no danger in sight. The Wild Boar replied: ". . . Won't have time to sharpen my tusks when danger comes."

The Farmer and the Ungrateful Snake

One day in winter a Farmer came across a Snake half-frozen from the cold. He took pity on the creature, picked him up, and put him inside his shirt. As soon as the Snake had warmed up he resumed his snakelike ways and sank his poisonous fangs into the man who had saved his life. The dying Farmer exclaimed: "I should have known better than to feel sorry for such a vile creature."

The Lion and the Wild Boar

In the heat of summer a Lion and a Wild Boar came to drink at a small spring. Each claimed the right to drink first; words led to blows and soon they were locked in combat. As they drew back for the final assault, the two animals caught sight of some vultures wheeling slowly overhead. Promptly their anger faded, for they agreed that it was better for them to make friends than to make a meal for the vultures.

The Sick Man and the Doctor

A Sick Man received a visit from his Doctor, who asked him how he was feeling. The patient replied that he was sweating more than usual. "Good sign!" said the Doctor.

On the second visit the Sick Man reported that he had had an attack of violent trembling. "Couldn't be better!" said the Doctor.

On the third visit the Sick Man was suffering from acute diarrhea. "Just the thing!" said the Doctor.

A little later one of his relatives asked how he was getting on. "I'm dying of good symptoms," sighed the Sick Man.

The Man Bitten by a Dog

A Man bitten by a mad Dog ran about in search of someone to treat his wound. A passerby told him that he should wipe away the blood with a crust of bread and feed it to the Dog who had attacked him. "But if I did that," the Man replied, "every Dog in town would try to sink his teeth into me!"

The Ant

The creature we know as the Ant was formerly a man. This man tilled the soil for a living, but he was never content with the fruits of his own labor; he constantly cast envious glances at his neighbors' fields and frequently stole into them to carry off their produce. Zeus, disgusted by his greed, changed him into an insect. But though his form is different, his character remains the same, for he still creeps through his neighbors' fields carrying off grains of wheat and barley that he hides away for his own use.

The Kid and the Flute-playing Wolf

A Kid who had strayed from the flock was suddenly set upon by a Wolf. The Kid turned to his attacker and exclaimed: "I am well aware, Mr. Wolf, that I shall be your dinner. But why don't we do the thing in style? Before dining, let us have a bit of music. You play your flute and I will dance." The Wolf played, the Kid danced, and the noise attracted a pack of dogs who instantly set upon the Wolf. The Wolf turned to the Kid and exclaimed: "It is only what I deserve. A competent butcher has no business playing the flute."

The Wolf and the Heron

A Wolf got a bone stuck in his throat and rushed about in search of help. He met a Heron and offered to pay him handsomely for extracting the bone. The Heron plunged his beak deep into the Wolf's throat, drew forth the bone, and claimed his fee.

"What!" exclaimed the Wolf, "isn't it enough that you recovered your head safe and sound from a Wolf's jaws, without asking for money as well?"

The Frogs Who Wanted a King

The Frogs, weary of the anarchic way in which they lived, sent a delegation to Zeus to ask for a King. Zeus, knowing them to be simpletons, tossed a stick of wood into their pond. Terrified at the commotion, the Frogs plunged to the bottom of the water; but when the stick showed no signs of moving, they came to the surface again. Soon they came to hold their monarch in such scorn that they did not hesitate to jump all over him. And not long after, they sent another delegation to Zeus, complaining that their present King was sluggish and requesting a replacement. Zeus, irritated by their pestering, sent down a hydra, who gobbled them all up.

The Wolf and the Lamb

The Wolf came across a Lamb drinking at a river and wanted an excuse to attack him. He accused the Lamb of muddying the water and making it not fit to drink. The Lamb replied that he was drinking as he had been taught, barely touching the water with his lips; moreover, he did not see how he could be bothering the Wolf, who was after all standing upstream. The Wolf, a bit taken aback by this reply, tried another tack. "Last year you played my father a nasty trick." "But I was not even born a year ago!" protested the Lamb. At which the Wolf exclaimed: "Well, you may be a pretty slick talker, but I'm going to eat you all the same."

The Bull and the Wild Goats

A Bull pursued by a lion took refuge in a cave inhabited by Wild Goats. Butted and gored by them, he exclaimed: "If I put up with your ill-manners, it is not because I fear you, but because I fear the animal who waits at the entrance of this cave."

The Ass Who Passed for a Lion

An Ass put on a Lion's skin, and men and beasts fled at his approach. A gust of wind, however, lifted the Lion's skin from his back, revealing what he was. Whereupon everyone ran up from all sides and kicked and clubbed him.

The Ant and the Dung Beetle

During the summer months the Ant scoured the fields for grains of wheat and barley against the coming winter. A Dung Beetle watched him at his work and expressed surprise that the Ant should put himself to such trouble at a time when other creatures were taking it easy and enjoying the good weather. The Ant answered not a word; but several months later, when the winter rains had washed away the manure and the hungry Dung Beetle came to beg alms of the Ant, he rebuked him thus: "Silly insect, if you had taken the trouble to exert yourself instead of mocking me at my labors, you would not now lack food."

The Ass Bearing an Idol

A man strapped a statue of a god to his Ass's back and led the beast into town. The people along the way bowed low before the Idol, and the Ass, imagining that their homage was directed at him, swelled with pride. He stood there in the middle of the road, refused to budge, and brayed at the top of his lungs. The Ass's owner guessed what was in the beast's mind and gave him a whack with a stick. "Poor imbecile," said the man. "A sorry state we will have come to when men take to worshipping Asses!"

The Fir Tree and the Bramblebush

The Fir Tree and the Bramblebush were having an argument. The Fir Tree boasted: "I am handsome, slender, tall, and I serve to make the roofs of temples and the hulls of ships. And what have you to say for yourself?" Replied the Bramblebush: "You have only to think a moment on the subject of saws and axes to appreciate why it is far better to be a Bramblebush."

The Thieving Child and His Mother

A Child stole some writing tablets from his schoolmates and brought them to his Mother who, instead of punishing him, praised him for his cleverness. He then brought her a stolen cloak and she praised him even more. Time passed; he grew bigger and his thefts kept pace with his growth. Finally, however, he was caught and led with his arms tied behind his back to the place of execution. His Mother accompanied him, wailing and beating her breasts. As the fateful moment approached, he asked permission to whisper a final message in her ear, and when she leaned toward him he sank his teeth into the ear and bit off the lobe. His Mother vehemently rebuked her son for his impiety: not content with his past crimes, he now saw fit to mutilate his own Mother! He answered: "If only you had seen fit to punish me when I stole those tablets, I would not now be facing death!"

The Boy in Danger of Drowning

A Boy went swimming by himself and suddenly started to flounder in the water. Seeing a passerby in the distance, he called out for help. The passerby began to scold him for swimming beyond his depth, but the Boy interrupted: "Save your scoldings until after you have saved me!"

The Rich Man and the Hired Mourners

A Rich Man had two daughters, and when one of them died he hired some women to mourn at her funeral. The other daughter protested to her mother: "It's really shameful: we are the ones who are bereaved, and yet these women, who couldn't care less, are crying and carrying on much louder than we are!" The mother replied: "That's nothing to be surprised about. The passion of these women is real enough, but it has to do with money, not with death."

Hermes' Chariot

One day Hermes filled his Chariot with lies, villainies, and sundry deceits, and started making the rounds of all the countries of the world. At each stop he distributed a small portion of his load, but when he reached Arabia his Chariot — so they say — broke down, and its entire contents were pillaged by the Arabs, who believed they were carrying off a great treasure.

The Shepherd Who Liked Practical Jokes

A Shepherd who tended his flock at some distance from the village took delight in the following Practical Joke. He would cry out that his sheep were being attacked by wolves, and when the villagers came running they would find the flock grazing peacefully on the hillside. One day the wolves really attacked the flock. The Shepherd sent up a great cry for help, but the villagers had at last learned their lesson and paid no attention. Meanwhile the flock was consumed to the very last sheep.

The Two Roosters and the Eagle

Two Roosters were fighting over the barnyard hens. One of them finally conceded defeat and fled to the bushes, where he hid himself away. The other flew to the top of a high wall and proclaimed his victory to the world. An Eagle promptly swooped down and carried him off, whereupon the other Rooster came out of hiding and tranquilly took possession of the harem.

The Ill-shorn Lamb

Turning her head to the man who was struggling to shear her, the Lamb said: "If it is my wool you are after, don't clip so close; but if it is my meat, then put an end to this torture and plunge your blade home!"

The Fox and the Monkey Who Was Elected King

At a great assembly of the animals the Monkey had so pleased the crowd by his dancing that he had been elected King. The Fox was jealous and, having found a piece of meat set out in a trap by hunters, he told the Monkey that he had discovered a treasure which belonged by rights to his lord and master — to, that is, the Monkey himself. The Fox led his sovereign to the place, and when the Monkey rushed forward to seize the meat he was caught in the trap. The Monkey accused the Fox of treason, but the Fox replied: "Such stupidity is hardly worthy of someone who claims to be King of the Animals."

The Miser

A Miser converted all his belongings into gold, melted the gold into one large lump, and buried the lump in a corner of his garden, along with his heart, soul, and tenderest concern. Every day he paid a visit to his treasure; and one day a neighbor guessed his secret, dug up the gold, and carried it away. The Miser, finding the treasure gone, began to wail and tear his hair. A passerby, on learning the cause of this performance, remarked: "There's no need to carry on so, my friend. When you had your gold, it was hardly yours. Why not take a rock, bury it right there, and pretend that it is the gold? It will surely serve just as well, for as far as I can tell even when you had the gold, you never had any use for it."

The Wall and the Battering Ram

A Wall received a nasty blow from a Battering Ram and cried out in alarm: "How can you treat me like this, when I have never done you any harm?" "Don't blame me," replied the Battering Ram, "blame the man who's got hold of me — he's doing the shoving."

The Tortoise and the Hare

The Tortoise and the Hare were arguing about who could run the faster. To end the dispute they decided to have a race. The Hare, confident of victory, was in no hurry to start. In fact, he lay down at the side of the road and went to sleep. The Tortoise, however, was well aware of his disadvantages, and crawled without a pause until he had far outdistanced the sleeping Hare and crossed the finish line before him.

The Crow and the Snake

A hungry Crow caught sight of a Snake asleep in a sunny hollow and swooped down on him. As he was carrying off his prey, the Snake twisted about and bit him. "What bad luck to die of a lucky find," moaned the Crow, and died.

The Flea and the Athlete

There was an Athlete who happened to be laid up, and a Flea jumped onto his toe and bit him. The angry Athlete tried to crush him with his fingernails, but the Flea was ready for him and with one bold jump escaped from his victim's clutches. The Athlete groaned and said: "O Heracles, patron and protector of athletes, if this is the sort of help you provide when I am struggling with a Flea, what can I expect from you when I meet my real adversaries?"

The Asses Complain to Zeus

The Asses sent a deputation to Zeus to complain about the endless toil and trouble that was their lot in life, and to request that he put an end to their labors. Zeus, in order to make clear the impossibility of such a thing, declared that he would grant their request when they had pissed enough to form a running river. The Asses, however, insisted on taking his statement literally, and from that day to this whenever they see one Ass pissing they all gather around to offer their own contributions.

The Hyena and the Fox

It is said that hyenas change their sex every year, becoming male and female by turns. A Hyena once reproached a Fox for rejecting her friendly overtures. "Don't blame me," said the Fox, "but Nature herself who makes it impossible for me to know whether I would be gaining a girlfriend or a pal."

The Wolf and the Old Woman

A hungry Wolf was prowling about in search of food when he heard an Old Woman shout at a child: "Stop that howling this minute or I'll tell the Wolf to take you away!" The Wolf, taking the Old Woman at her word, decided to wait for developments. At dusk, the Wolf crept closer to the house and heard the Old Woman crooning to the child: "Go to sleep, little one. If ever that naughty Wolf comes round, we'll chase him away." Whereupon the Wolf took himself off, muttering that "At this farm people say one thing and do another!"

Diogenes and the Bald Man

Diogenes, the philosopher, was insulted by a Bald Man and replied: "I am certainly not going to engage in an exchange of insults; on the contrary, I shall sing the praises of all those many hairs that had the good sense to desert a wicked head."

The War Between the Rats and the Weasels

The Rats and the Weasels went to War. The Rats, who were clearly getting the worst of things, held a council of War and decided that the fault lay with their leadership. New generals were therefore selected by popular vote; and these new generals, anxious to differentiate themselves from the common soliders, fashioned themselves elaborate headdresses with decorative horns. When warfare resumed, the Rats were once again routed and hastily withdrew into their holes; all of them, that is, except their new leaders, whose horns were too large to allow them to enter, and who were consequently captured and devoured.

The Lioness and the Fox

A Fox referred disparagingly to the fact that the Lioness gave birth to only one cub at a time.

"Only one," replied the Lioness, "but a lion."

The Reed and the Olive Tree

The Reed and the Olive Tree were arguing. Each claimed to be stronger, sturdier, to have greater endurance than the other. The Olive Tree jeered at the Reed for bowing down to every passing breeze — to which the Reed made no reply. But a little later a windstorm blew up and the Reed, bending before the wind, came through easily whereas the Olive Tree, which defiantly faced the violent blast, was uprooted and destroyed.

The Two Sacks

When Prometheus fashioned man, he hung Two Sacks around his neck. The first Sack contained the faults of other men, the second the faults of the wearer himself. The god saw fit to hang the first Sack in front, but the second he let dangle behind. And that is why man is quick to notice the faults of others, but never sees his own.

The Travelers and the Crow

A group of men traveling together on business met with a Crow who had only one eye. One of the group read the bird as an ill omen and advised his companions to return home. But another man spoke out: "How can this bird possibly predict our future when he could not even foresee the accident which cost him his eye?"

The Eagle Wounded by an Arrow

An Eagle was perched on a ledge scanning the ground for rabbits when a hunter hit him with an Arrow. The Arrow pierced his breast and its end, with the quivering feathers, stuck out before the Eagle's very eyes. At that sight the great bird exclaimed: "What could be worse than to be killed by one's own weapons!"

The Dove and the Crow

A Dove brought up in a dovecote was boasting of her many offspring. A Crow cut her off with the remark: "It is not children you are raising but slaves."

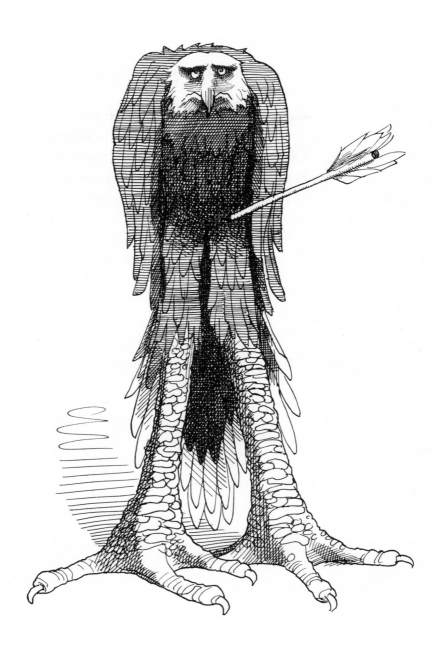

The Horse and the Soldier

For the duration of the war a Soldier fed his Horse on the best oats and, in short, treated him like a true comrade-in-arms. When, however, the war ended, the Horse was made into a beast of burden, set to hard labor, and given only hay to eat. Once again war broke out; the Soldier bridled his Horse, took up his arms, and started off to battle. But the half-starved Horse stumbled at every step and finally exclaimed: "You had better join the ranks of the foot-soldiers, for you have made your Horse into an ass, and there's no way of changing an ass back into a Horse."

The Dancing Camel

A Camel who was forced to dance by his owner remarked: "Well, I may look pretty silly dancing, but then, I look silly when I walk too."

Finis